NEW FRONTIERS
EXPLORATION IN THE 20th CENTURY
THE ARCTIC AND ANTARCTIC
CASS R. SANDAK

FRANKLIN WATTS
NEW YORK LONDON TORONTO SYDNEY

Cover photograph courtesy of the National Science Foundation/Russ Kinne./Back cover photograph courtesy of Allyn Baum/Monkmeyer Press Photo Service, Inc./Photograph on title page courtesy of U.S. Department of the Navy.

Photographs courtesy of: Emil Schulthess/Black Star: pp. 4, 21 (bottom), 23 (top right), 25 (bottom left); Ivan Jirak/Monkmeyer Press Photo Service, Inc.: p. 5 (top); National Science Foundation/Ann Hawthorne (Division of Polar Programs): pp. 5 (bottom), 20 (right), 21 (top), 23 (bottom left), 25 (top), 26, 27 (top left); New York Public Library Picture Collection: pp. 6 (left), 7 (left) photo by Frank Nowell, 18 (bottom) photo by George Holton; Dr. Owen Beattie, The University of Alberta: p. 6 (right); U.S. Department of the Navy Photo: pp. 7 (right), 8 (middle), 11 (top), 17, 19 (top), 20 (left); Archives of The Explorers Club: p. 8 (top); The Granger Collection, New York: p. 8 (bottom); U.S. Naval Historical Center Photo: pp. 9 (top), 10 (bottom); APN/Frank Spooner Pictures: p. 9 (bottom); C.L. Andrews Collection in the Archives, Alaska and Polar Regions Department, University of Alaska, Fairbanks: p. 10 (top); Figaro/Frank Spooner Pictures: p. 11 (bottom left); Galissian/Frank Spooner Pictures: p. 11 (right); Anchorage Convention and Visitors Bureau: pp. 12 (top), 13 (top); Jack Lentfer/Survival Anglia Ltd.: p. 12 (left); Joel Bennett/Survival Anglia Ltd.: pp. 12 (bottom right), 13 (bottom); © William Curtsinger/Photo Researchers, Inc.: pp. 14 (left), 22; Lamont-Doherty Geological Observatory of Columbia University, Hunkins et al.: p. 14 (right); © Joe Rychetnik/Photo Researchers, Inc.: p. 15 (left); Institute of Polar Studies, The Ohio State University: p. 15 (right); Royal Norwegian Embassy Information Service: p. 16 (top); the author: pp. 16 (bottom), 18 (top); National Archives: p. 19 (bottom left); David Moore/Black Star: p. 19 (right); © William Curtsinger/Science Source/Photo Researchers, Inc.: p. 23 (top left); National Science Foundation/Russ Kinne: pp. 23 (bottom right), 24 (bottom), 25 (bottom right), 27 (top right); © Doug Allan/Science Photo Library/Photo Researchers, Inc.: pp. 24 (top), 27 (bottom); Tass from Sovfoto: p. 28 (left); U.S. Air Force Photo: p. 28 (right); E.I. DuPont De Nemours and Company, Inc.: p. 29 (top); Mobile Photo Library: p. 29 (bottom).

FOR DAWN

First published in the USA
by Franklin Watts Inc.
387 Park Ave. South
New York, N.Y. 10016

First published in 1987 by
Franklin Watts
12a Golden Square
London W1R 4BA

First published in Australia
by Franklin Watts
Australia
14 Mars Road
Lane Cove, NSW 2066

US ISBN: 0-531-10137-1
UK ISBN: 0-86313 470 X
Library of Congress
Catalog Card No: 86-50386

Designed by Michael Cooper

TABLE OF CONTENTS

THE POLAR REGIONS

Some 20,000 km (12,500 mi) separate the North Pole from the South Pole. The North Pole, or Arctic region, is at the top of the world; the South Pole, or Antarctica, is at the bottom. The name Arctic comes from the Greek word for bear, *arctos*, because it is the Little Bear constellation that includes Polaris, the North Star, or Pole Star, that is over the North Pole. In contrast, Antarctica means "opposite the bear," in other words, at the opposite, or southern, end of the globe.

The Arctic and Antarctic regions are bitterly cold and forbidding. Many geographers describe the areas within the Arctic and Antarctic Circles as the Frigid Zones. They are among the last places on Earth to be explored. Despite the dangers, these regions have long fascinated explorers and adventurers. Although they share many similarities, there are plenty of differences, too.

The Arctic region consists mostly of the Arctic Ocean, which is surrounded by the northernmost parts of North America, Eurasia, Greenland, and several northerly islands. The North Pole itself is in the middle of the Arctic Ocean. The ocean is covered with ice that ranges from a few feet to more than 30 m (100 ft) in thickness. The Arctic ice cap is a disk of floating ice. Depending on the season, it can be as much as 1,600 km (1,000 mi) across. Winds, tides and currents keep this ice in slow but constant motion.

Unlike much of the Arctic, the region known as Antarctica is mostly solid land. In fact, Antarctica is the fifth largest continent. It is about twice the size of Australia, and it lies almost entirely within the Antarctic Circle. Antarctica is separated from the rest of the world by stormy seas, unscalable mountains, and cliffs of ice that are almost impassable. Antarctica is a very cold and unwelcoming place.

A signpost at Antarctica's McMurdo Station points the way to the North Pole and other far-off places.

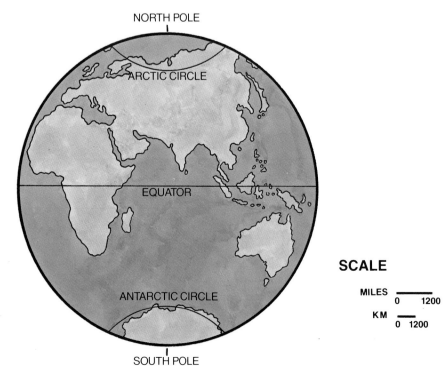

SCALE

MILES
0   1200

KM
0   1200

On the coast of Canada's Baffin Island, within the Arctic Circle, a lone worker sets up camp during the long Arctic night. Wind has sculpted the ice and snow into wave-like sastrugi.

Adelie penguins survey the rugged Antarctic coast of southern Victoria Land. Some penguins can dive down to 265 m (800 ft) and stay submerged for as long as 15 minutes.

The lowest temperatures ever recorded on the Earth's surface have been measured in Antarctica. In 1960 a temperature of $-88.4°C$ ($-127°F$) was registered at the USSR Vostok Station. Sometimes it is so cold that metals can shatter like glass. An unprotected person could freeze solid in minutes.

The race to conquer these regions has been one of the greatest adventure stories of the twentieth century. Polar exploration has developed as adventurers have looked for new and shorter routes around the globe or have sought to fill in gaps in our knowledge of the Earth's terrain. Until the early years of this century no explorer had reached the North or South Poles. In recent years, many of the explorers have been scientists—people who have traveled to the ends of the Earth to learn more about weather, magnetic forces, geology and plant and animal life. Many of them have come to uncover new resources, deposits of coal, oil and metals and minerals useful for industry, medicine and defense.

LOOKING NORTH

For several centuries adventurers had been pressing northward, trying to find northern sea passages between the Atlantic and Pacific oceans. The Northeast Passage was the first of these new trade routes to be found. In 1878–79, the Swede Nils Nordenskjold sailed through the passage that European navigators had been hunting for centuries. Earlier Nordenskjold had tried unsuccessfully to reach the North Pole using reindeer-drawn sleds, but these were hampered by rough ice.

In earlier times some explorers expected to be able to sail through an ice-free Arctic Ocean to reach the North Pole. They reasoned—incorrectly—that a huge body of salt water could not remain frozen. The area surrounding the North Pole is, in fact, made up of water and ice—nearly 15.5 million sq km (6 million sq mi) of frozen or partly frozen sea. Huge icebergs and ice floes drift through the water, where currents of varying temperature create ice of differing thickness and stability.

From 1845 to 1847 the British Sir John Franklin led an expedition in search of the Northwest Passage across Canada to the Orient. He came within a few miles of reaching his goal but the party was lost, presumably in a storm. More than forty rescue teams were sent after the party. Even today relics are still being found.

In 1895 the Norwegian Fridtjof Nansen came within 386 km (240 mi) of the North Pole. A naturalist by training, he studied magnetism; the temperature and salinity of the sea water; the formation, growth and thickness of ice; ice temperatures at different levels; currents around and under the ice; electricity in the air; and the aurora borealis, or northern lights. He monitored his crew members carefully. Each month during their long stay in the Arctic, he weighed them and took blood samples.

Below left. **An early view of Novaya Zemlya, discovered by the Dutch explorer William Barents in 1597.** Below. **In 1984 modern explorers found the body of Petty Officer John Torrington, a member of Franklin's lost party.**

Nansen, his crew and his ship, the *Fram* (which means "forward"), endured the harshness of the Arctic weather and sailed farther north than any other people had sailed at that time. Although he and his crew left the *Fram* and went even farther north on foot, they never reached the North Pole.

Most importantly Nansen proved once and for all that the Arctic region was essentially an ocean basin and that the North Pole was situated in the middle of the frozen sea. His meticulous studies of Arctic meteorology laid the foundations for future exploration in the region.

The Norwegian Roald Amundsen, on board the *Gjoa*, was the first navigator who successfully sailed through the Northwest Passage above Canada's northern territories on a voyage from 1903 to 1906. Today the coastal waters of northern Alaska, which he was first to navigate, are among the richest oil fields in the world. But for many explorers the real prize was the North Pole itself.

Above left. **Amundsen's ship, *Gjoa*.** Above. **In 1969 the modern icebreaker-tanker *Manhattan* re-created the earlier voyage of the *Gjoa*.**

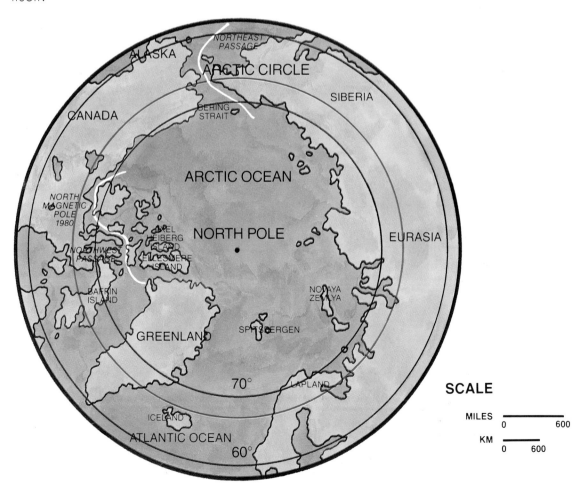

SCALE

MILES 0 — 600

KM 0 — 600

7

PEARY AND AFTER

Commander (later Admiral) Robert Edwin Peary, an American, made a series of attempts to reach the North Pole. He devoted twenty-three years of his life to achieving his goal. In his attempts he lost two companions and nine of his own toes to the bitter North. By 1905 Peary had come within 289 km (180 mi) of the Pole aboard the reinforced American steamer *Roosevelt.* Peary was a very determined man, so he kept on trying.

Peary had to plan his Arctic assault for early springtime, when days of increasing sunlight made the frozen north a more hospitable place but before the sun melted too much ice. Later in the season the spring tides would cause much of the ice to break up and make travel even more hazardous.

The North Pole is separated from the nearest land masses— Ellesmere Island and Greenland—by 664.5 km (413 mi). Peary's point of departure was Cape Columbus on Ellesmere Island. He and his party began the dash on March 1, 1909. In all, the party was made up of twenty-four men, nineteen sleds and 133 dogs. Six separate teams were assigned to help with different portions of the journey.

Peary found that the biggest obstacles to travel across the frozen ocean were pressure ridges, where the sea has heaved blocks of ice together to form high barriers. Even more frightening were channels of black open water, called leads, where wind and tide have caused the floating blocks of ice to separate. A lead could swallow up a manned dog team in seconds, sending all to a watery grave. Peary's final attempt to reach the North Pole was frequently delayed by these leads, some of which the party crossed on rafts of ice. The threat of storms was ever present, and there was always the danger of frostbite in the bitterly cold temperatures.

Top. **Matthew Henson, Peary's assistant.** Above. **Peary adopted multilayered Eskimo (Inuit) clothing as the most effective way of surviving in the Arctic.** Below left. **A postcard showing Peary and Dr. Frederick A. Cook, who claimed he had reached the North Pole in 1908. Investigators rejected the claim.**

In his years of exploration in the Arctic, Peary had learned the secrets of survival in the North. He chose the best diet for hard work in the region. Pemmican—lean meat, which is dried and powdered and mixed with fat—was an invention of the North American Indians. It is high in calories and protein. Peary called it "the most satisfying food I know."

On April 6, 1909, Peary succeeded in accomplishing what all earlier explorers had failed to do. Peary, his black assistant Matthew Henson, and four Eskimo guides—Ootah, Egingwah, Seeglo and Ooqueah—became the first people to reach the North Pole.

Successive journeys by many later explorers helped to piece together an increasingly accurate map of the Arctic region. Islands and passages that earlier expeditions had reported were found not to exist. The Danish explorer Knud Rasmussen's crossing of Greenland in 1912 proved that Peary's earlier outline map of northeast Greenland was wrong. And Donald Macmillan, an American who from 1913 to 1917 retraced many of Peary's journeys, proved that Crockerland, an island Peary claimed to have sighted north of Axel Heiberg Island, did not even exist.

The American flag is raised at the North Pole in 1909.

Dogsleds are still one of the best ways to travel in the Arctic. This dog team led the way on a modern expedition across the USSR to connect the west with the east. Using teams of dogs not unlike these, the Peary party made the 780 km (485 mi) return trip from the pole to Ellesmere Island in only 16 days, a record in itself.

GETTING AROUND

During the 1920s, air flight and radio communication significantly expanded the possibilities for Arctic exploration. In 1926 Admiral Richard E. Byrd was the first person to complete a flight over the North Pole. In 1925 Roald Amundsen and Lincoln Ellsworth took off in their two polar-flight flying boats from Spitsbergen, but head winds kept them from reaching the North Pole. George Binney, another aviator, organized three Oxford University scientific expeditions, during which radio was used in the Arctic for the first time.

Two famous expeditions brought dirigibles to the Arctic. In 1926 the *Norge* carried Amundsen and the Italian Umberto Nobile from Europe to America in a flight over the North Pole. Two years later, Nobile's own dirigible, *Italia*, reached the Pole but met with disaster on the return flight. The airship was forced down by severe wind. The gondola, with Nobile and its crew, broke away on the ice as the airship itself rose into the air and was never seen again.

The veteran polar explorer Amundsen lost his life in the rescue effort. Nobile was later saved by a Swedish plane, and two of his men were rescued independently. The true story of what happened has never been revealed, but ugly and conflicting rumors of murder, dereliction of duty and even cannibalism plagued Nobile and the other survivors until the end of their days.

The *Norge* had two 250-hp engines that carried the vessel during windless conditions.

On May 9, 1926, Richard E. Byrd flew from Spitsbergen to the North Pole and back again in sixteen hours.

A recent nuclear submarine, *Queenfish*, breaks through the polar ice. The open water at the bottom of the picture is called a polynya.

In 1931 the Australian-born Captain G.H. Wilkins tried to reach the North Pole by submarine. His attempt helped to pave the way for later submarine expeditions, including that of the world's first nuclear-powered submarine, the *Nautilus*. Nuclear submarines are ideal for Arctic exploration because they can make lengthier voyages and stay submerged longer than conventional subs.

The US Navy's *Nautilus* crossed the Arctic from the Pacific to the Atlantic in 1958. Near Alaska the vessel submerged under the pack ice and successfully pursued a perilous underwater journey. It finally reached the area beneath the North Pole on August 3. Here the *Nautilus* took measurements and discovered that the ice cap extended 8.3 m (25 ft) below the surface of the ocean. The water temperature was a chilly 0°C (32.4°F) and the sea bottom was 4,470 m (13,410 ft) beneath the Pole. A short time later, another American nuclear submarine, the *Skate*, broke through the ice and surfaced at the Pole.

Today's Arctic explorers can use the same means of travel as earlier adventurers—dogsleds, ships and aircraft. But they also have helicopters, powerful icebreakers and many types of all-terrain vehicles, such as the snowcat. This vehicle is equipped with treads for easy maneuvering on the ice and special clawlike grips for climbing steep ridges and icy slopes.

Below left. **A Polish icebreaker in search of the North Magnetic Pole in 1981–82.** Below. **A modern expedition crosses Greenland in a specially equipped truck.**

LIFE IN THE NORTH

Explorers have told us much about life in the frozen North. Temperatures are cold all year long, but in the summer, in July, they are sometimes well above freezing and can even get quite warm. There are dense fog banks. Pack ice and ice floes form when the sea freezes.

Glaciers are enormous rivers of thick, dense ice that has built up over years and even centuries. They may cover hundreds of square miles of land. As glaciers move they scour the land with their tremendous weight. When they reach the edge of the sea the ice breaks off, or calves, forming icebergs. In the summer this calving occurs with loud reports that sound like thunder. Icebergs may be a mile or more long and tower hundreds of feet above the ocean's surface.

In the winter the average temperature is well below freezing, and the winter months are almost completely without daylight. At the Arctic Circle for months on end the sun merely peeps over the horizon for a brief time each day. At the Pole itself almost complete darkness lasts for six months, and in the areas between the North Pole and the Arctic Circle the average is four months. In summer the midnight sun circles the horizon without setting.

Because the weather is so severe, the land areas within the Arctic Circle are largely treeless. Even in summer only the upper layer of topsoil thaws out to allow plants to grow. Several inches beneath this layer is the permafrost, a layer of ground that is frozen the year round.

A large portion of the land that circles the Arctic Ocean is tundra—bare soil and rock covered with mosses, lichens and low growth—that supports wildlife and incredible numbers of insects. In the summer this land is a region of lush grasses and flowering plants. In northern Europe and Asia the tundra provides rich pasture for the herds of reindeer (known as caribou in North America). Hares and lemmings as well as various species of voles and mice also make their homes in the tundra.

A "totem pole" made up of frozen oil pipeline valves shows the modern world arriving in the Arctic.

A walrus (left) and polar bear (right). They are both examples of animals unique to the Arctic region.

The animals of the Arctic are designed for survival under wintry conditions. The arctic fox sheds its white fur in the summer and then will appear brownish against the tundra. Polar bears think nothing of rolling and playing in the snow, but they are also adventurous: they will swim 24 to 32 km (15 to 20 mi) through open water to find new hunting grounds.

The Arctic Ocean teems with microscopic animals. Algae grow there from March until late autumn, and they are the basis of the food chain in the Arctic. Large aquatic mammals—narwhals, walruses, whales and many species of seals—are found there, although hunters threaten their existence.

The Inuit (Eskimos) of North America and Greenland are not the only human inhabitants of the Arctic region. The Lapps of northern Europe and the Chukchi of northeastern Siberia are also hardy survivors. They have endured some of the most difficult living conditions on Earth, yet they have moved into the modern world, keeping old traditions while sharing in today's advanced technology.

Knud Rasmussen was born in Greenland of partial Eskimo extraction himself. He spent thirty years exploring the Arctic and studying Eskimos. Vilhjalmur Stefansson was a Canadian explorer of Icelandic background. From 1913 to 1918 he remained north of the Arctic Circle for more than five years, in the longest single sustained polar expedition ever undertaken.

Musk oxen on the Arctic coast of Alaska.

13

STUDYING THE REGION

Much of today's exploration in the Arctic is carried out by scientists who want to learn more about the region. These scientists have developed special techniques and sensitive equipment that will survive in the cold. This equipment measures and records a wealth of data regarding the environment at the northern end of the Earth.

Scientific expeditions at the North Pole today have many different objectives. Mapping and charting continues, usually from plane or satellite images. Geologists try to piece together the natural history of the region and look for resources.

Oceanographers measure air and water temperatures, obtain water samples from all depths, track Arctic Ocean currents and take depth soundings to chart the bottom of the Arctic Ocean basin. An echo sounder allows scientists to measure the depth to which ice descends below the surface of the sea.

The North Pole is the best place to study the Earth's gravitational and magnetic fields. It is also a good place to study the shape of the Earth itself—geodetic measurement. Arctic meteorology has worldwide implications, especially on atmospheric circulation in the northern hemisphere.

Many strange effects of light are seen at the North Pole. Mirages are caused by the refraction of sunlight in dense, cold air. Interactions of fog and atmospheric ice crystals can create other types of optical illusions.

Below left. **Divers set up a sub-igloo on the Arctic sea floor.** Below. **A photograph of the Arctic sea floor more than 3.2 km (2 mi) below the ice cap.**

The splendid colors of the northern lights (aurora borealis) illuminate the night sky. The auroras are caused by electrically charged particles from the sun striking nitrogen and oxygen in the ionosphere—from 80 to 965 km (50 to 600 mi) above the Earth. This causes them to glow with an eerie light that can shimmer across the night sky like a giant curtain. Sun dogs and moon dogs are halo-like effects that light up the polar sky.

Glaciology is the study of ice and its formation and movement. Among the lands that encircle the Arctic Ocean are many islands, with countless inlets that have been sculpted by huge glaciers. Glaciologists take precise measurements of ice temperature, thickness, density, composition and movement. Often, movement of the ice must be measured from space with astronomical instruments because there are so few fixed features of landscape in the frozen north.

In the past, individual expeditions gathered most of the information about the Arctic. Exploration today is carried out at permanent or semipermanent stations where scientists collect and monitor data over long periods of time.

In the late 1930s, the Soviets, led by Ivan Papanin, pioneered setting up scientific stations on ice floes in the Arctic Ocean. Soon the United States undertook the same type of research. Aircraft drop off scientific crew members and necessary equipment on the ice floe. The team of scientists sets up living quarters and a research station there. They can continue their experiments for months or even a year or two until the ice floe begins to break up. Satellites track the movements of the floating stations and relay information to computer data centers.

Left. **Biologists study polar life forms and how they adapt to the climate. Here a biologist weighs an Alaskan polar bear.** Above. **Meteorological Station at Casement Glacier, Alaska. Setting up permanent stations near the North Pole, where there are few landmasses, presents special problems.**

RACING SOUTH

After Peary had reached the North Pole, a mad scramble began among nations and explorers to be the first to get to the South Pole. After 1900 in almost every year at least one new expedition was mounted or an existing one continued. For centuries the Arctic region had excited people looking for northerly trade routes. But interest in the South Pole, thousands of miles from civilization and the nearest human beings, lagged far behind, largely because the area was so inaccessible.

Antarctica is a remote area 965 km (600 mi) from the nearest part of South America. During the Antarctic winter, which lasts from March to December, the continent is virtually unapproachable by sea. The ice extends far out from the land's edge, and there are no warming currents to moderate the climate.

Antarctica was almost completely unknown before the twentieth century. Whalers began hunting in Antarctic waters in the early nineteenth century. In 1820 Edward Bransfield, a British naval officer, Captain Fabian von Bellingshausen, a Russian explorer who circumnavigated Antarctica, and Nathaniel Palmer, an American sealer, all discovered the continent at virtually the same time.

Early explorers faced a frozen and hostile world. Ice floes crushed ships, cracks opened in the ice and swallowed men and dog teams and blizzards wrecked many expeditions. Storms, starvation and the bitter cold all took their toll.

In a four-year expedition, from 1839 to 1843, James Ross discovered and named Ross Island and the Ross Ice Barrier, and the active volcano, Mount Erebus. In 1872–76 the *Challenger* expedition carried out important ocean research in the waters near the Antarctic Circle. But it was not until the *Belgica* expedition in 1897 that explorers actually set out to explore the Antarctic continent itself through a complete cycle of seasons.

Roald Amundsen. Careful planning, a swift dog team and skis helped him become the first person to reach the South Pole.

Scott's party at the South Pole on January 18, 1912. On the return journey, the party was lost in a blizzard. Scientists are still finding remains and records of the expedition and as recently as 1986 some food samples were uncovered.

A diver works through a hole in the sea ice to study undersea life near McMurdo Station. Mount Erebus is in the background.

And no one had yet gone as far as the South Pole. The rugged terrain remains one of the particular difficulties in Antarctic exploration. There are glacier-covered mountains ranging from 3,350 to 5,180 m (11,000 to 17,000 ft). Even if the snow were stripped away, the average elevation (1,830 m, or 6,000 ft) is nearly twice that of the other continents.

One of the most exciting and dangerous adventures began in 1911, when Robert F. Scott, a veteran British polar explorer, set out to reach the South Pole. He arrived at the Pole in January of 1912, only to find that a Norwegian flag had been raised there just thirty-five days earlier by Roald Amundsen. The Norwegian explorer had been the first person to reach the South Pole, on December 14, 1911. The disheartened Scott and his companions perished on the trek back.

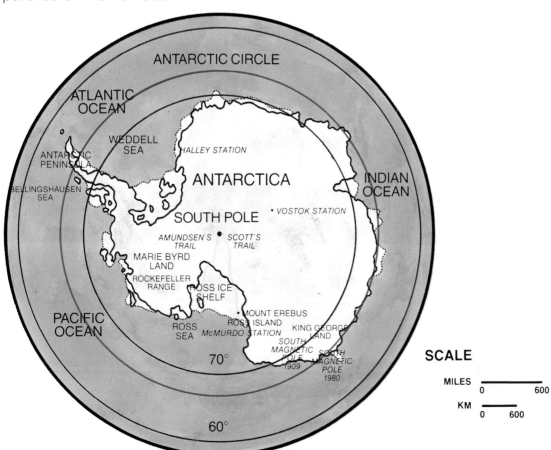

STAYING ON

Ernest Shackleton had been a member of Scott's 1901–04 Antarctic expedition, and like many polar explorers he couldn't seem to stay away from the frozen continent. In 1907–09 he had commanded his own expedition, using sturdy Manchurian ponies instead of dogs. But only 155 km (97 mi) from the Pole the last of his ponies fell into a crevasse, and Shackleton had to abandon his attempt to become the first to reach the South Pole. The journey wasn't a complete failure, though, since members of the expedition located the South Magnetic Pole and also climbed Mount Erebus.

On a later expedition, in 1914–17, Shackleton's ship, the *Endurance,* was crushed by ice and slowly sank. He led five of his men in an open boat over 1,280 km (800 mi) to safety on South Georgia Island. A little more than four months later he returned to rescue the rest of his group, who had almost given up hope. Shackleton died and was buried on South Georgia in 1922.

An exciting new era of Antarctic exploration began in 1928 with Sir G.H. Wilkins, the first person to introduce planes and aerial photography to Antarctica. His role was then taken up by Douglas Mawson, an English explorer who led expeditions for Australia. A member of Shackleton's 1907–09 team, he later led an Australian expedition and discovered King George Land in 1911–14. From 1929 to 1930 he surveyed 1,600 km (1,000 mi) of uncharted coast in a seaplane and mapped large sections of Antarctica that had only been vaguely known before.

Airplanes were the biggest boon to exploration of the continent, since they allowed people and supplies to be carried hundreds of miles inland while ships had a difficult time even nearing the shore. Planes could also scout icebound seas and report dangerous iceberg sightings. But there are hazards, too. Whiteout is the inability to distinguish ground from air, and it can be a problem to polar aircraft. Storms can come up suddenly, and compasses are unreliable so close to the South Pole.

Shackleton's ship, the *Endurance,* was crushed by ice while still 560 km (346 mi) from land.

Shackleton's base camp at Cape Royds. The dry air and extreme cold have left the building perfectly preserved.

Richard E. Byrd made a total of five Antarctic expeditions by plane between 1929 and 1956, during which he saw more than 25% of the continent. Byrd added more geographic knowledge of Antarctica than all of his predecessors combined.

By far the most important aircraft explorer was the American Richard E. Byrd. In 1929 he first visited Antarctica, where he discovered the Rockefeller mountain range and established the research station "Little America." Later that year he returned and flew over the South Pole on November 28, 1929.

Byrd's aerial reconaissance flights made use of a special photographic technique in which five cameras were used simultaneously. They photographed the same quadrants of ground from different angles at the same time, while a separate camera kept a permanent record of instrument readings. This gave them a panoramic view of the continent from several different perspectives.

In the 1930s, the Soviets established a base some 900 km (560 mi) from the South Pole. In May 1937 four Russian aviators piloted a plane to within 24 km (15 mi) of the South Pole, where they set up a camp. There they remained stranded until February of 1938.

Below left. **One of the early photographs taken of members of the Byrd party building a camp.** Below. **Today's aviation mapping units are capable of photographing hundreds of square miles in one day. The air is often clear enough to photograph objects 350 km (210 mi) away.**

LEARNING MORE

Today's Antarctic explorers have modern equipment that makes their work easier than it was in the past, but some obstacles remain. The severe cold is ever present. Winds of 80 to 160 km/h (50 to 100 mph) frequently sweep across the frozen landscape, and gales of 320 km/h (200 mph) are not uncommon. Crevasses are deep cracks or openings in the ice covered over by deceptive layers of snow that only mask the dangers. They are a threat to all Antarctic explorers.

During the British Commonwealth Trans-Antarctic Expedition, from 1955-58, the first coast-to-coast land crossing of Antarctica was made. Just two years after conquering Mount Everest, Sir Edmund Hillary led a team from New Zealand who set up supply depots at measured distances from their starting point at the Scott Base on the Ross Ice Shelf. Hillary's party of New Zealand explorers reached the South Pole on January 3, 1958. At the same time, Dr. Vivian Fuchs led a team from the Shackleton Base on the Weddell Sea inland to the South Pole. He reached the Pole on January 20, 1958.

After spending two days at the South Pole, Fuchs continued on to the Scott Base, which he reached five weeks later on March 2. He had completed his crossing of the continent in ninety-nine days, covering a total distance of 3,500 km (2,180 mi). Throughout the expedition a team of scientists collected geological and glaciological data. Ice-depth soundings were taken with seismic equipment and precise measurements of the Earth's magnetic field were made. They benefited from knowledge gained in more than a century of polar exploration.

Below left. **Hillary and Fuchs meet Rear Admiral George Dufek of the US Navy 3.2 km (2 mi) from the South Pole in 1958.**
Below. **Geophysicists lower dynamite into a crevasse on Ross Island at the base of Mount Erebus. The crampons on their boots help give them firmer footing. The explosion will provide a seismic reading to indicate the thickness of the ice.**

A marine biologist collects samples from the underside of the ice and from the bottom of the ocean.

A glaciologist's pit. Scientists can learn much by studying layers of ice and snow.

Explorers had learned a good deal about Antarctica in the early years of the twentieth century, but many details remained undiscovered until 1957–58, the International Geophysical Year. During IGY, scientists set up fifty-five research stations on Antarctica and the islands that surround it. Biologists, oceanographers, physicists, chemists, geologists, meteorologists and glaciologists participated in collecting and sharing data.

Since IGY, the number of permanent stations has been reduced but their facilities have been greatly improved. A treaty signed in 1961 guarantees neutrality and ensures cooperation in Antarctic territory. Today there are forty permanent stations staffed year round by scientists from the member nations of this treaty. The aim of the treaty is to set aside the claims of individual countries and to preserve Antarctica as a vast laboratory for international scientific study. The treaty is due for renewal in 1991.

Most of the research stations are in clusters around the edges of the continent, where the temperatures are somewhat warmer than at the Pole itself. India, Brazil and the International Greenpeace Organization plan to set up permanent research stations before the 1980s are over.

LIFE OUTDOORS

Many of today's explorers are scientific researchers and for them the Antarctic provides a spotless laboratory with ideal conditions for many experiments. The air is so pure that mountain peaks can often be seen hundreds of miles away. Low temperatures help to achieve a nearly sterile environment. Bacteria, which swarm in temperate lands, are almost nonexistent in Antarctica. Some studies have found a single bacterium per pint of snow. These are conditions similar to outer space.

Although there are no permanent human residents of Antarctica, there is a complex web of life that includes large and flourishing populations of the relatively few species that live there. Scientists have identified just over sixty species of animals living on land or in the sea south of the Antarctic Circle.

Most of the continent is covered with a sheet of ice 2,000 m (6,000 ft) thick, and in some places the ice is even more than 3.2 km (2 mi) thick. Because of the cold and the short growing season, the most successful plants are simple ones: algae, lichens and mosses. A few Antarctic plants can complete their life cycles and reproduce in a period of as little as five days. Hardy grasses have made a toehold on sunny rocks in the ice-free valleys. These phenomena, along with occasional ice-free lakes, presumably heated by thermal springs, still puzzle scientists.

Antarctica supports a surprisingly rich array of animals and fish that are unique in their adaptations to the cold weather. There are the well-known penguin, seagull and seal. There are very few insects and the only one of any significance is a tiny mosquito. The skua, a type of large bird, preys on penguin eggs and babies and also feeds on krill, the tiny shrimplike organisms upon which whales feed.

A marine biologist studies a bellowing elephant-seal calf. Early whalers almost caused extinction of these pugnacious animals, whose weight averages 2,300 kg (5,000 lb).

Far left. **A tracking device on a gentoo penguin measures the bird's activities and the effects of the cold weather on the animal.** Left. **Seals like this one were hunted by the earliest Antarctic explorers for their valuable fur.**

The coastal waters of Antarctica swarm with plankton—microscopic plants and animals that support krill. Satellites can monitor plankton levels and show the migrations of whales and fish.

Dinoflagellates are single-cell planktonic plants that move by means of their whiplike tails. Explosive population growth of these tiny organisms causes the sea to turn red, resulting in a phenomenon known as "red tide." Toxins produced by the animals can poison fish and shellfish and may be a problem for commercial fisheries.

Scientists have discovered that the livers of some Antarctic fish, including Antarctic cod, manufacture a type of "antifreeze" that blocks the formation of ice crystals. Body fluids will not freeze when the fish swim through super-chilled waters.

In the layers of rocks in Antarctic mountains paleontologists have recently found fossils of many species of reptiles and amphibians. All of these animal remains date from a time when Antarctica enjoyed a much warmer climate and had thick forests. Scientists believe that the land that is now the Antarctic continent drifted to the bottom of the world from a position near the Equator.

Below left. **A marine biologist studies rare fossilized shells from New Harbor on the mainland.** Below. **Algae on the surface of Lake Bonney.**

SCIENCE TODAY

The pioneer age of Antarctic exploration is past, and there are probably no new land features left to discover. But the places already known are yielding up their secrets to the scientists, technicians and other adventurers who seek to add to our knowledge of the region. Antarctica's uniqueness as a laboratory makes it ideal for scientific experiments.

Oceanographers study and plot the flow of offshore currents. Antarctica is circled by an eastward-moving current that is the world's largest and has a speed of half a knot. Roughly 1,600 km (1,000 mi) away from Antarctica, the continent is surrounded by a 40-km-wide (24 mi) zone of water known as the Antarctic Convergence. This area acts almost as a barrier that keeps the cold Antarctic waters from mixing with the warmer waters northward in the Atlantic, Pacific and Indian oceans.

Geologists and glaciologists study the depth of the ice and the rock formations beneath it. They also measure the accumulation of ice and snow. Antarctica holds about 95% of the world's ice, and 65% of the world's fresh water is locked up in it. Glaciologists study the ice with a Rammsonde, an instrument with a conical metal point. The point is driven through successive layers of snow and ice. It measures the density of the layers and helps scientists determine the rate of its accumulation.

Geophysicists come to Antarctica to conduct experiments and to take precise measurements of the Earth's magnetic field and of cosmic radiation. Satellite information has revealed a growing "hole" in the ozone layer that protects the Earth from harmful radiation. In 1986 the South Magnetic Pole was relocated. Because of atmospheric conditions, its position shifts about 8.8 km (5.5 mi) each year, and it has been identified at various sites over the years. The 1986 location placed it 150 km (93 mi) off the coast, north of the French Dumont D'Urville research station.

Technicians building the aerial mast for the British Antarctic Survey's Halley Station, an advanced ionospheric sounder project. Many studies of climate and sea level change are being carried out.

Geologists drill for granite cores in Antarctica.

A solar telescope is a common sight near McMurdo Station.

In Antarctica scientists can find the quietest seismic region in the world. Because it has the least vibration and earthquake activity, Antarctica is a perfect place to monitor earthquake and volcanic activity around the world.

The study of plate tectonics has allowed scientists to develop a reasonable theory of the continent's origins and past development. Geophysicists say that the Antarctic plateau is similar to the terrain of Africa. They believe that Antarctica was probably once joined to Africa, India and South America when all the landmasses of the southern hemisphere formed one huge landmass called Gondwanaland. Because parts of Africa are rich in minerals, scientists think Antarctica may also yield rich supplies. Coal, copper, nickel and other minerals have been found there, but large-scale mining is still far from practical, because conventional equipment will not function in the harsh climate.

Because Antarctica was once a warm continent teeming with plant and animal life, many geologists now believe that huge untapped oil resources lie beneath Antarctica's continental shelf. Developing commercial resources in this supercold environment presents difficulties. The efforts to overcome these obstacles could permanently alter and damage the Antarctic environment and lead to territorial disputes among countries.

Below left. **A scientist measures magnetism in a laboratory under the ice.** Below. **The crater of Mount Erebus, one of the continent's five active volcanoes. The "smoke" is actually water vapor from the hot air which rises from the volcano and hits the cold air.**

AN ANTARCTIC STATION

Visitors to the Antarctic are struck by the eerie silence; some say that the quiet is deeper and more ominous there than in any other place on Earth. Sometimes the only sound that can be heard hundreds of miles from civilization is the wind.

Space inside most Antarctic research stations is very cramped, and there is almost no privacy. Like life aboard a submarine, where crew members are crowded together and isolated from the outside world often for weeks at a time, life at an Antarctic station can be very tedious.

Days and nights that are four months long can confuse the body's normal biological rhythms unless a strict discipline is kept. Every effort is made to simulate normal living conditions, and it is important to keep a regular routine. This helps to maintain spirits and also to avoid such problems as insomnia and exhaustion.

Fresh water is at a premium since it takes so much fuel and energy to melt ice and snow to make water for bathing. Most people are asked to take only two brief showers a week, but the cold temperatures and dry air make more frequent bathing unnecessary.

The lifestyle is not all grim, however. The men and women who work at the Antarctic find time for reading and hobbies: working out in a gymnasium or playing all kinds of games. VCRs make recent films and TV programs available.

Doors on buildings are like the heavy doors on meat storage lockers; they are designed to keep out the cold. The temperatures in the snow-covered tunnels that connect the buildings of a station are often −33°C (−60°F). At that temperature the air can freeze the capillaries in the bronchial tubes that lead into the lungs.

An aerial view of McMurdo Station. A city by itself, the base includes living quarters, a post office and a church as well as a nuclear power station. McMurdo has a population of 800 to 1,000 in the summer and about 100 in winter.

Psychologists find Antarctica a perfect laboratory for studying stress and isolation. Depression and aggression are just a few of the disorders that doctors have observed. Other problems include drug and alcohol abuse. Some people may lose weight because they are not used to the frigid conditions, but the opposite is more likely to occur: people eating more than usual to compensate for frustration and boredom. For many people *the* welcome alternative is work.

The men and women who live and work at the bottom of the world must endure months of darkness; there are other times when the sunlight is so blinding that it can cause problems unless eyes are protected with special sunglasses. Some scientists feel that living and working in Antarctic stations is good training for the harsh conditions that exist in outer space.

Indoors and outdoors: A football game on the sea ice (left) is a good contrast to the barracks-like confinement (above) of the living quarters. This juggler is inside a jamesway, a tent made of canvas in an arch shape. Jamesways are modular units that serve as living areas in Antarctica.

An aerial view of the living modules set inside wooden tubes at the British Halley Station base, built in 1983. The wooden tubes are specially built to withstand the pressure of heavy snow.

TODAY AND TOMORROW

The spirit of adventure is very much alive. Even today explorers are still making history in the polar regions. In 1978 Naomi Uemura, traveling alone, reached the North Pole by dogsled. In January 1986, a British exploration vessel, the *Southern Quest*, was crushed in the ice and sank in Antarctic waters. At almost the same time a team of British explorers successfully retraced Scott's 1912 route to the South Pole. And three separate groups of mountaineers set about scaling the peaks of the Vinson Massif, Antarctica's highest range.

Another major polar challenge was completed during the years 1979 to 1982, when two Britons—Sir Ranulph Fiennes and his companion, Charles Burton—went to the South Pole on skis, snowshoes and in snowmobiles. They traveled north and navigated the Northwest Passage before returning home to England. They became the first people to circle the globe from pole to pole and covered five continents and 84,000 km (52,000 mi).

From the mid-nineteenth century onward the Russians have expressed keen interest in the Arctic because so much of their land is close to the Arctic Circle. Other nations in the northern hemisphere share a concern that Soviet holdings and domination in the Arctic may cause future political struggles. Antarctica also has strategic significance.

Many people have big plans for the polar regions. Nuclear power is helping to push back the natural frontiers. It is an efficient and inexpensive source of heat, light and power for communities in the polar regions. Futurists dream of supplying the deserts with fresh water by towing icebergs to where they are needed. Others plan huge domes of glass that could shelter whole camps in a greenhouse-like atmosphere. Russian scientists have proposed a scheme to spray the polar ice with black powder that will absorb the sun's warmth and melt it.

Modern technology comes to the poles. Below left. **The Soviet icebreaker *Moskva* speeds on its way to a rescue mission.** Below. **A Defense Early Warning (DEW) station, part of a system that stretches across the Arctic.**

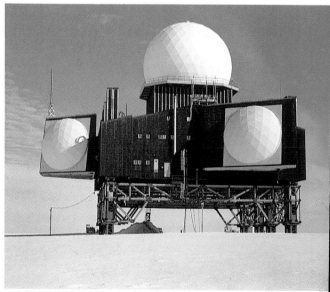

The six triumphant members of the 1986 team who reached the North Pole. They are holding the Minnesota state flag, since three of the team were from that state. Two of the original members had to be flown back to the United States earlier because of injuries.

Scientists are eagerly watching for satellite data showing changes in the size of the polar ice caps because of the importance of these findings on world climate. With the gradual warming of the Earth by the Greenhouse Effect, as solar radiation is absorbed by carbon dioxide in the atmosphere and is held there, melting ice could cause sea levels around the world to rise by as much as 60 m (200 ft), flooding cities and coastal areas.

But there is also a closer future. Already the Chilean government offers special premiums to families that settle in Antarctica for a period of years. They hope this will help ensure their territorial claims if the continent is ever divided up.

Development and pollution are the two biggest threats to polar stability at the moment. The dream is that both the Arctic and Antarctic will be set aside for peaceful scientific research. That way their beauty will be maintained and military and territorial ambitions will have no place. But as scientists uncover the riches of the polar regions, governments become eager to exploit them. The great hope for the future is that the poles will stay unpolluted and that all the people of the world will be able to share in their resources.

Prince Charles (right) and Ranulph Fiennes (far left) flank naval officers as Fiennes returns to England after completing the voyage that took him from pole to pole.

DATELINES

ARCTIC

1903–06 In his ship the *Gjoa*, Roald Amundsen becomes the first person to navigate the Northwest Passage.

1908–09 Robert E. Peary reaches the North Pole on April 6, 1909.

1915 Russian Admiral Vilkitski navigates the Northeast Passage from Siberia to Europe.

1926 Richard E. Byrd and Floyd Bennett fly from Spitsbergen to the North Pole and back.

1928 Umberto Nobile and the *Italia* are lost in an effort to fly a dirigible over the North Pole. Nobile is rescued, but Amundsen loses his life during a rescue attempt.

1931 Hubert Wilkins attempts to cross the Arctic Ocean in a submarine called the *Nautilus*.

1958–59 Another submarine named *Nautilus*, this one nuclear powered, crosses from the Pacific to the Atlantic under the North Pole. Later the *Skate* surfaces there.

1968–69 Wally Herbert and the British Trans-Arctic Expedition cross the polar ice cap, using dogs.

1978 Naomi Uemura of Japan, traveling alone, reaches the North Pole by dogsled.

1981–82 Sir Ranulph Fiennes and his team travel pole to pole on the British Transglobe Expedition.

1986 Eight separate parties set out to reach the North Pole. Six fail in the attempt. Will Steger and his group of five men and one woman reach the Pole. The Frenchman Jean-Louis Etienne skis to the North Pole alone. Three US Navy submarines surface at the North Pole.

ANTARCTIC

1901–04 The British National Antarctic Expedition, led by Commander Robert F. Scott, sails to McMurdo Sound in the *Discovery*.

1901–09 Ernest Shackleton leads the British Antarctic Expedition and winters at Cape Royds, Ross Island. They come within 160 km (97 mi) of the South Pole.

1911 Roald Amundsen and five men reach the South Pole on December 14.

1912 Scott and his party reach the South Pole on January 17, just one month after Amundsen. But the party perishes on the return journey.

1914–17 Shackleton's British Imperial Trans-Antarctic expedition meets with near disaster. The ship *Endurance* sinks.

1928–29 Sir Hubert Wilkins introduces aerial photography to Antarctica.

1929 Richard E. Byrd is the first to fly over the South Pole on November 28 on the earliest of his airborne expeditions.

1955–58 Hillary and Fuchs lead British Commonwealth Trans-Antarctic Expedition on first land crossing of the Antarctic.

1957–58 International Geophysical Year. Twelve nations establish 55 stations on the continent.

1961 The Antarctic Treaty is signed. It is due for renewal in 1991.

1979–81 British Transglobe Expedition's Antarctic crossing by Sir Ranulph Fiennes and his party.

1986 Tins of food left behind by the ill-fated Scott expedition are found.

GLOSSARY

AURORA A shimmering glow caused by charged particles in the upper atmosphere. The northern lights (aurora borealis) and southern lights (aurora australis) are examples.

CALVING The breaking away of huge chunks of ice from glaciers that reach the sea.

CRAMPONS Plates with metal spikes attached to shoes to give better traction on ice.

CREVASSE A deep vertical crack or split in a glacier or ice sheet, often hidden under accumulated snow.

FLOE A piece of free-floating sea ice. Floes may be 16 km (10 mi) or more in diameter.

FRIGID ZONES The geographic areas between the Arctic Circle (at the North) and the North Pole. At the South the frigid zone is between the Antarctic Circle and the South Pole.

FROSTBITE The freezing of a portion of the body.

GEODETIC Relating to the size and shape of the Earth and its magnetic and gravitational fields.

GLACIER A mass of moving snow and ice that has built up over a period of many years.

GLACIOLOGY The study of ice and the formation and movement of ice.

HYDROGRAPHY The study of bodies of water.

HYPOTHERMIA Dangerously low body temperature caused by prolonged exposure to cold.

ICEBERG A large block of floating sea ice which has broken off from a glacier or ice shelf.

ICE CAP A dome-shaped mass of ice that covers land.

ICE SHEET A large ice cap, usually covering more than 50,000 sq km (20,000 sq mi).

ICE SHELF A thick sheet of floating ice attached to land. The edge of the Ross Ice Shelf of Antarctica has cliffs as high as 60 m (200 ft) and stretches for more than 650 km (400 mi).

LEAD An area of open water through floating ice.

MAGNETIC POLES The shifting poles of the Earth's magnetic field. They are nonstationary points in the general region of the North and South poles. Compasses point to them rather than to the geographic poles.

MIDNIGHT SUN The nighttime sunlight that shines during the Arctic and Antarctic summer.

MOON DOGS Halo-like light effects seen at the Poles. During the day they are seen as sun dogs.

PACK ICE Any floating sea ice that is not attached to land. Sometimes it forms huge sheets that break up into floes or smaller pieces.

PERMAFROST The layer of soil just beneath the topsoil in the Arctic. Even in summer this layer of ground remains frozen.

PLANKTON Tiny plants and animals that live and float in seawater.

PRESSURE RIDGE A wall of floating ice fragments forced upward under pressure.

RED TIDE Seawater discolored by an overabundance of dinoflagellates which die off, producing red toxins.

TUNDRA The treeless land, mostly soil and rock, of the Arctic region. It is usually covered with mosses and other low growth.

WHITEOUT The condition when sunlight is diffused and no shadows are cast. It is almost impossible to distinguish between sky and land, since there is no visible horizon.

INDEX